COOKING FOR FRIENDS

SUPERCOOK'S KITCHEN

D0552799

Marshall Cavendish London & New York

Picture Credits

Theo Bergstrom: 74
Alan Duns: 8, 16, 22, 34, 72, 80, 82, 90, 94
Jerry Harpup: 42
Paul Kemp: 18, 24, 26, 56
Mike Leale: 14
David Meldrum: 38
Roger Phillips: 4, 6, 10, 12, 20, 28, 30, 36,
    40, 44, 46, 48, 50, 52, 60, 64, 66, 68, 76,
    78, 84, 86, 88, 92
Iain Reid: 54, 58, 62, 70

Recipes: Norma McMillan
House editor: Isabel Moore

Published by
Marshall Cavendish Books Limited
58 Old Compton Street
LONDON W1V 5PA

Printed in Great Britain

ISBN 0 85685 728 9

CONTENTS

Cockle soup

Metric/Imperial

48 cockles, cooked and cooking
  broth reserved
50g/2oz butter
15g/½oz flour
600ml/1 pint milk
30ml/2 tbs. chopped parsley
2 celery stalks, chopped
15ml/1 tbs. lemon juice
60ml/4 tbs. double cream

American

48 cockles, cooked and cooking
  broth reserved
¼ cup butter
2 tbs. flour
2½ cups milk
2 tbs. chopped parsley
2 celery stalks, chopped
1 tbs. lemon juice
¼ cup heavy cream

Remove the cockles from their shells. Melt the butter in a saucepan. Add the flour and cook, stirring, for 1 minute. Gradually stir in the milk and strained cockle broth and bring to the boil, stirring. Add the parsley, celery, lemon juice and seasoning to taste and cook for 10 minutes.

Add the cockles and cream and cook gently for a further 2 to 3 minutes or until the cockles are heated through. **SERVES 6**

Fish soup

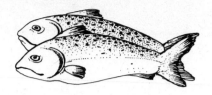

Metric/Imperial

75ml/3floz olive oil
2 large onions, chopped
4 garlic cloves, crushed
3 leeks, chopped
6 spring onions, chopped
½kg/1lb tomatoes, skinned, seeded
 and chopped
15ml/1 tbs. tomato purée
5ml/1 tsp. fennel seeds
1 bouquet garni
1¼kg/2½lb prepared fish (mullet,
 bass, whiting and Dublin bay
 prawns), chopped
600ml/1 pint water
250g/8oz crabmeat, flaked

American

⅓ cup olive oil
2 large onions, chopped
4 garlic cloves, crushed
3 leeks, chopped
6 scallions, chopped
1lb tomatoes, skinned, seeded
 and chopped
1 tbs. tomato paste
1 tsp. fennel seeds
1 bouquet garni
2½lb prepared fish (mullet, bass,
 whiting and jumbo shrimp),
 chopped
2½ cups water
½lb crabmeat, flaked

Heat the oil in a saucepan. Add the onions, garlic, leeks and spring onions (scallions) and fry until softened. Stir in the tomatoes, tomato purée (paste), fennel seeds, bouquet garni and seasoning to taste. Simmer for 5 minutes.

Add the fish and water and bring to the boil. Simmer for 15 minutes, stirring occasionally. Add the crabmeat and simmer for a further 5 minutes or until all the fish is tender. **SERVES 4-6**

Asparagus cream soup

Metric/Imperial	American
1kg/2lb asparagus	*2lb asparagus*
1 small onion, sliced	*1 small onion, sliced*
900ml/1½ pints light stock	*2 pints light stock*
25g/1oz butter	*2 tbs. butter*
25g/1oz flour	*¼ cup flour*
2 egg yolks	*2 egg yolks*
150ml/¼ pint single cream	*⅔ cup light cream*

Cut off the asparagus tips and reserve. Cut the stalks into 5cm/2in pieces. Put the stalk pieces, onion and stock in a saucepan and bring to the boil. Cover and simmer for 30 minutes.

Meanwhile, cook the asparagus tips gently in simmering salted water for 5 minutes or until they are tender. Drain.

Purée the asparagus stalk mixture and return to the saucepan. Season to taste and reheat. Mix the butter and flour together to make a paste (beurre manié) and add to the soup in small pieces, stirring. Simmer until thickened.

Mix together the egg yolks and cream. Add a little of the hot soup, then return to the pan. Heat through gently. Do not boil. Add the asparagus tips and serve hot. **SERVES 4**

Petite marmite

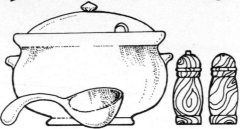

Metric/Imperial

1 chicken carcass
½kg/1lb topside of beef, cut into
  1cm/½in pieces
1.8 litres/3 pints beef consommé
2 carrots, shredded
1 turnip, shredded
2 leeks, shredded
1 onion, finely chopped
2 celery stalks, shredded
½ small white cabbage, cored
  and shredded
175g/6oz cooked chicken breast
  meat, shredded

American

1 chicken carcass
1lb top round of beef, cut into
  ½in pieces
4 pints beef consommé
2 carrots, shredded
1 turnip, shredded
2 leeks, shredded
1 onion, finely chopped
2 celery stalks, shredded
½ small white cabbage, cored
  and shredded
1 cup shredded cooked chicken
  breast meat

Put the chicken carcass and beef in a marmite (earthenware pot) or saucepan and pour over the consommé. Bring to the boil and boil for 5 minutes, skimming any scum that rises to the surface. Add all the vegetables. Cover and simmer for 2 to 2½ hours or until the beef is tender.

Remove and discard the chicken carcass. Stir the chicken meat into the soup and heat through gently. **SERVES 4-6**

Gazpacho

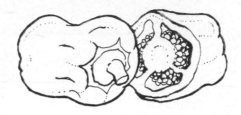

Metric/Imperial

3 slices of brown bread, cubed
300ml/½ pint tomato juice
2 garlic cloves, minced
½ cucumber, peeled and finely
  chopped
1 green pepper, cored, seeded
  and finely chopped
1 red pepper, cored, seeded
  and finely chopped
1 large onion, finely chopped
¾kg/1½lb tomatoes, skinned,
  seeded and chopped
75ml/3floz olive oil
30ml/2 tbs. wine vinegar
1.25ml/¼ tsp. dried marjoram
1.25ml/¼ tsp. dried basil

American

3 slices of brown bread, cubed
1¼ cups tomato juice
2 garlic cloves, minced
½ cucumber, peeled and finely
  chopped
1 green pepper, cored, seeded
  and finely chopped
1 red pepper, cored, seeded and
  finely chopped
1 large onion, finely chopped
1½lb tomatoes, skinned, seeded
  and chopped
⅓ cup olive oil
2 tbs. wine vinegar
¼ tsp. dried marjoram
¼ tsp. dried basil

Soak the bread cubes in the tomato juice for 5 minutes. Squeeze them to remove excess liquid and transfer to another bowl. Reserve the tomato juice.

Add the garlic, cucumber, peppers, onion and tomatoes to the bread. Purée in a blender, or pound to a paste with a pestle and mortar, or rub through a strainer or food mill. Stir in the reserved tomato juice, oil, vinegar, herbs and seasoning to taste. The soup should be the consistency of single (light) cream, so if necessary add more tomato juice. Chill well.

Drop a few ice cubes into the soup and serve with croutons and chopped cucumber, hard-boiled (hard-cooked) egg and olives.

SERVES 4

Chicken liver pâté

Metric/Imperial	American
1 celery stalk	*1 celery stalk*
3 parsley sprigs	*3 parsley sprigs*
8 peppercorns	*8 peppercorns*
½kg/1lb chicken livers	*1lb chicken livers*
2.5ml/½ tsp. Tabasco sauce	*½ tsp. Tabasco sauce*
250g/8oz butter	*1 cup butter*
1.25ml/¼ tsp. grated nutmeg	*¼ tsp. grated nutmeg*
10ml/2 tsp. dry mustard	*2 tsp. dry mustard*
1.25ml/¼ tsp. ground cloves	*¼ tsp. ground cloves*
1 medium onion, minced	*1 medium onion, minced*
1 garlic clove, minced	*1 garlic clove, minced*
30ml/2 tbs. brandy	*2 tbs. brandy*
50g/2oz stuffed olives, sliced	*½ cup sliced stuffed olives*

Half fill a saucepan with water and bring to the boil. Add the celery, parsley and peppercorns and simmer for 10 minutes. Add the chicken livers, cover and simmer for a further 10 minutes. Drain the livers and mince (grind) them. Add the Tabasco, butter, nutmeg, mustard, cloves, onion, garlic, brandy and salt to taste to the livers and mix together thoroughly.

Press the liver mixture into a serving dish and decorate the top with the olive slices. Chill for at least 6 hours before serving.   **SERVES 8**

Cheese pâté

Metric/Imperial	American
750ml/1¼ pints milk	1½ pints milk
1 large onion, chopped	1 large onion, chopped
1 large carrot, chopped	1 large carrot, chopped
2 celery stalks, chopped	2 celery stalks, chopped
1 bouquet garni	1 bouquet garni
75g/3oz butter	6 tbs. butter
75g/3oz flour	¾ cup flour
45ml/3 tbs. mayonnaise	3 tbs. mayonnaise
10ml/2 tsp. lemon juice	2 tsp. lemon juice
3 garlic cloves, crushed	3 garlic cloves, crushed
10 stuffed olives, finely chopped	10 stuffed olives, finely chopped
pinch of cayenne	pinch of cayenne
350g/12oz Stilton or other blue cheese, rind removed, crumbled	¾lb Stilton or other blue cheese, rind, removed, crumbled

Scald the milk, then add the onion, carrot, celery and bouquet garni. Cover and simmer for 15 minutes. Remove from the heat and allow to cool, then strain the milk.

Melt the butter in the cleaned-out saucepan. Add the flour and cook, stirring, for 2 minutes. Gradually stir in the milk and bring to the boil, stirring. Simmer until thickened. Remove from the heat and cool.

When the sauce is cool, beat in the mayonnaise, lemon juice, garlic, olives, cayenne and seasoning to taste. Rub the cheese through a strainer, then beat it into the sauce mixture.

Spoon the paté into a serving dish. Chill until set.   **SERVES 8-10**

Spinach ring

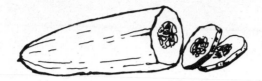

Metric/Imperial

¾kg/1½lb spinach, cooked, drained
  and chopped
½ cucumber, finely chopped
6 spring onions, chopped
2.5ml/½ tsp. dried marjoram
1.25ml/¼ tsp. dry mustard
15g/½oz gelatine
45ml/3 tbs. hot water
425ml/14floz chicken stock
30ml/2 tbs. cider vinegar

American

1½lb spinach, cooked, drained
  and chopped
½ cucumber, finely chopped
6 scallions, chopped
½ tsp. dried marjoram
¼ tsp. dry mustard
2 envelopes unflavored gelatin
3 tbs. hot water
1¾ cups chicken stock
2 tbs. cider vinegar

Mix together the spinach, cucumber, spring onions (scallions), marjoram, mustard and seasoning to taste. Dissolve the gelatine in the water and mix with the stock and vinegar. Stir into the spinach mixture. Pour into a dampened 1.2 litre/2 pint (2½ pint) capacity ring mould. Chill until set.

Turn out of the mould to serve. If liked, fill the centre with a prawn (shrimp) cocktail mixture.   **SERVES 4-6**

Grapefruit & orange appetizer

Metric/Imperial	American
2 medium grapefruit, peeled and segmented	2 medium grapefruit, peeled and segmented
1 large orange, peeled and segmented	1 large orange, peeled and segmented
½ cucumber, halved and sliced	½ cucumber, halved and sliced
mint sprig	mint sprig
DRESSING	**DRESSING**
45ml/3 tbs. corn oil	3 tbs. corn oil
2.5ml/½ tsp. lemon juice	½ tsp. lemon juice
5ml/1 tsp. sugar	1 tsp. sugar

Mix together the grapefruit and orange segments in a salad bowl. Arrange the cucumber slices decoratively around the fruit.

Mix together the dressing ingredients with seasoning to taste and pour over the fruit. Chill for 30 minutes. Serve garnished with a mint sprig.   **SERVES 4**

CANAPES

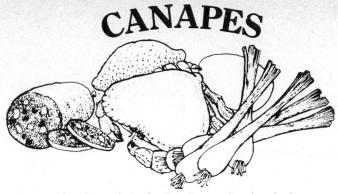

Crab canapés: fry a little finely chopped onion in butter until soft, then stir in 15ml/1 tbs. flour followed by 175ml/6floz ($\frac{3}{4}$ cup) cream. Cook, stirring, until thickened. Add 250g/8oz flaked crabmeat, a dash of Tabasco sauce, 5ml/1 tsp. lemon juice and seasoning to taste. Spread this mixture over 18 toast fingers. Beat together 15ml/1 tbs. cream cheese, 25g/1oz (2 tbs.) butter and 2.5ml/$\frac{1}{2}$ tsp. paprika. Put a dot of this on each toast finger and grill (broil) for 1 minute. Serve hot garnished with capers.

Salami canapés: place thin slices of salami on buttered circles of toast. Garnish with gherkin (pickle) fans.

Sardine canapés: mash together 1 can of sardines (drained of oil), 2.5ml/$\frac{1}{2}$ tsp. lemon juice, 10ml/2 tsp. chopped parsley and pepper to taste. Spread on 4 buttered slices of white bread (crusts removed) and cut each into 4 squares. Garnish each with a slice of hard-boiled (hard-cooked) egg and a rolled anchovy fillet.

Shrimp canapés: melt 50g/2oz ($\frac{1}{4}$ cup) butter in a saucepan and add 75g/3$\frac{1}{2}$oz canned shrimps (drained), 1.25ml/$\frac{1}{4}$ tsp. mild curry powder, pinch each of cayenne and chilli pepper, juice of $\frac{1}{4}$ lemon and salt to taste. Cook for 4 minutes. Spread on 12 small fried bread ovals. Garnish with chopped parsley.

Spinach canapés: cook $\frac{3}{4}$kg/1$\frac{1}{2}$lb spinach, then drain and chop it finely. Mix in 25g/1oz (2 tbs.) butter, 50g/2oz grated cheese and seasoning to taste. Spread on triangles of fried bread and sprinkle over more grated cheese and dry breadcrumbs. Grill (broil) for 2 to 3 minutes.

Tomato canapés: put slices of tomato on crisp savoury biscuits (crackers) and pipe a star of cream cheese mixed with garlic and parsley on top.

Paté canapés: arrange small squares of paté on buttered rectangles of brown bread and garnish with olive slices.

Smoked salmon canapés: put slices of smoked salmon on buttered diamonds of brown bread and garnish with lemon and parsley.

FISH

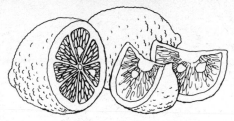

Salmon steaks florentine

Metric/Imperial
4 salmon steaks, about 2.5cm/
  1in thick
250g/8oz butter, melted
1kg/2lb spinach
60ml/4 tbs. double cream
juice of ½ lemon
pinch of cayenne
4 lemon slices

American
4 salmon steaks, about 1in
  thick
1 cup butter, melted
2lb spinach
¼ cup heavy cream
juice of ½ lemon
pinch of cayenne
4 lemon slices

Preheat the grill (broiler).
Season the salmon steaks and grill (broil) for 8 to 10 minutes on each side or until cooked through. Baste them with 50g/2oz (¼ cup) of the butter while they are cooking.
Meanwhile, cook the spinach. Drain it well and return to the pan. Stir in the cream and seasoning to taste. Keep hot.
Mix the lemon juice and cayenne into the remaining butter. Season to taste.
Spread the spinach on a warmed serving platter. Place the salmon steaks on top and pour over the butter sauce. Garnish with lemon twists.

SERVES 4

Trout with almonds

Metric/Imperial	American
6 medium trout	6 medium trout
30ml/2 tbs. lemon juice	2 tbs. lemon juice
100g/4oz flour	1 cup flour
5ml/1 tsp. grated nutmeg	1 tsp. grated nutmeg
1.25ml/¼ tsp. dried thyme	¼ tsp. dried thyme
175ml/6floz milk	¾ cup milk
150g/5oz butter	⅔ cup butter
100g/4oz slivered almonds	1 cup slivered almonds
parsley sprigs	parsley sprigs
lemon wedges	lemon wedges

Rub the fish with 15ml/1 tablespoon of the lemon juice and salt and pepper. Mix the flour with the nutmeg and thyme. Dip each fish first in the milk and then in the flour mixture to coat on all sides.

Melt 75g/3oz (6 tablespoons) of the butter in a frying pan. Add the fish and fry for 4 to 6 minutes on each side or until cooked through. Transfer them to a warmed serving platter and keep hot.

Add the remaining butter to the pan. When it has melted, stir in the almonds. Fry, stirring, for 3 to 4 minutes or until they are lightly browned. Pour them over the trout and garnish with parsley sprigs and lemon wedges. **SERVES 6**

Mullets with tomatoes & peppers

Metric/Imperial

6 medium mullets
juice of 1 lemon
75g/3oz ground pine nuts
2 garlic cloves, crushed
1 small onion, chopped
60ml/4 tbs. chopped parsley
45ml/3 tbs. olive oil
1 medium green pepper, cored,
  seeded and sliced
6 tomatoes, skinned, seeded and
  sliced
25g/1oz butter
6 black olives

American

6 medium mullets
juice of 1 lemon
½ cup ground pine nuts
2 garlic cloves, crushed
1 small onion, chopped
¼ cup chopped parsley
3 tbs. olive oil
1 medium green pepper, cored,
  seeded and sliced
6 tomatoes, skinned, seeded
  and sliced
2 tbs. butter
6 black olives

Sprinkle the fish with the lemon juice and leave to marinate for 15 minutes.

Preheat the oven to 180°C/350°F, Gas Mark 4.

Mix together the pine nuts, garlic, onion, parsley and seasoning to taste. Gradually beat in the olive oil.

Remove the fish from the lemon juice and pat dry. Arrange in a baking dish in one layer and spread over the pine nut mixture. Arrange the green pepper slices on top and cover with the tomatoes. Dot with the butter.

Place the dish in the oven and cook for 25 minutes or until the fish is tender. Transfer to a warmed serving platter. Put an olive in the uppermost empty eye socket of each fish.

SERVES 6

Sole bonne femme

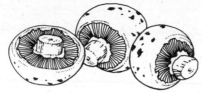

Metric/Imperial	American
¾kg/1½lb sole fillets, skinned	1½lb sole fillets, skinned
100g/4oz button mushrooms, chopped	¼lb button mushrooms, chopped
2 shallots or spring onions, finely chopped	2 shallots or scallions, finely chopped
120ml/4floz dry white wine	½ cup dry white wine
120ml/4floz fish stock	½ cup fish stock
15ml/1 tbs. lemon juice	1 tbs. lemon juice
1 bouquet garni	1 bouquet garni
25g/1oz butter	2 tbs. butter
15g/½oz flour	2 tbs. flour
30ml/2 tbs. double cream	2 tbs. heavy cream
12 mushroom caps, sautéed in 25g/1oz butter	12 mushroom caps, sautéed in 2 tbs. butter

Preheat the oven to 180°C/350°F, Gas Mark 4.

Rub the sole fillets with seasoning to taste. Arrange the chopped mushrooms and shallots on the bottom of a greased casserole. Place the sole fillets on top, folding them in half if necessary. Pour in half the wine, the stock and lemon juice and add the bouquet garni. Cover and put the casserole into the oven. Cook for 15 to 20 minutes or until the fish flakes easily. Transfer the fish to a warmed serving dish. Keep warm. Strain the cooking liquid into a jug.

Melt the butter in a saucepan. Add the flour and cook, stirring, for 1 minute. Gradually stir in the strained cooking liquid and the remaining wine and bring to the boil, stirring. Simmer until smooth and thickened. Stir in the cream and adjust the seasoning.

Pour the sauce over the fish and garnish with the mushroom caps.

SERVES 6

Cod with shrimp sauce

Metric/Imperial	American
25g/1oz butter	2 tbs. butter
1 onion, finely chopped	1 onion, finely chopped
100g/4oz mushrooms, sliced	¼lb mushrooms, sliced
4 tomatoes, skinned and chopped	4 tomatoes, skinned and chopped
¾-1kg/1½-2lb cod fillets, skinned	1½-2lb cod fillets, skinned
175ml/6floz dry white wine or fish stock	¾ cup dry white wine or fish stock
2 egg yolks	2 egg yolks
120ml/4floz double cream	½ cup heavy cream
15ml/1 tbs. lemon juice	1 tbs. lemon juice
100g/4oz shelled shrimps	¼lb shelled shrimp

Melt the butter in a frying pan. Add the onion and fry until softened. Stir in the mushrooms, tomatoes and seasoning to taste. Lay the fish fillets on top of the vegetables and pour over the wine or stock. Bring to the boil, then cover and simmer for 10 minutes or until the fish is cooked.

Transfer the fish to a warmed serving platter and keep hot. Boil the liquid in the frying pan until it has reduced by half. Beat the egg yolks and cream together. Stir in a little of the hot liquid, then stir into the liquid in the pan with the lemon juice. Cook gently for 3 to 4 minutes, stirring. Add the shrimps and cook for a further 2 to 3 minutes to heat through.

Pour the sauce over the fish and serve garnished with lemon slices and chopped parsley.

SERVES 6

Halibut with tomatoes

Metric/Imperial
25g/1oz butter
1 onion, sliced into rings
400g/14oz canned tomatoes,
  chopped
5ml/1 tsp. dried marjoram
4 halibut steaks
250g/8oz small button mushrooms,
  halved
150ml/¼ pint double cream

American
2 tbs. butter
1 onion, sliced into rings
14oz canned tomatoes,
  chopped
1 tsp. dried marjoram
4 halibut steaks
½lb small button mushrooms,
  halved
⅔ cup heavy cream

Melt the butter in a saucepan. Add the onion and fry until softened. Stir in the undrained tomatoes, marjoram and seasoning to taste. Bring to the boil, then add the halibut steaks. Cover and cook for 10 minutes, or until the fish is tender.
Stir in the mushrooms and cream and cook gently for a further 2 to 3 minutes to heat through.   **SERVES 4**

Lobster salad

Metric/Imperial	American
meat from 2 x ¾kg/1½lb lobsters, cubed	meat from 2 x 1½lb lobsters, cubed
250g/8oz shelled shrimps	½lb shelled shrimp
1 small pineapple, peeled, cored and chopped	1 small pineapple, peeled, cored and chopped
1 medium green pepper, cored, seeded and shredded	1 medium green pepper, cored, seeded and shredded
300g/10oz cooked long-grain rice	4 cups cooked long-grain rice
6 large radishes, sliced	6 large radishes, sliced
250ml/8floz mayonnaise	1 cup mayonnaise
dash of Tabasco sauce	dash of Tabasco sauce
10ml/2 tsp. paprika	2 tsp. paprika
75ml/3floz double cream, whipped	⅓ cup heavy cream, whipped
lettuce leaves	lettuce leaves
4 hard-boiled eggs, sliced	4 hard-cooked eggs, sliced
4 tomatoes, sliced	4 tomatoes, sliced
chopped chives	chopped chives

Mix together the lobster, shrimps, pineapple, pepper, rice and radishes. In another bowl combine the mayonnaise, Tabasco, paprika, seasoning to taste and cream. Add to the lobster mixture and toss well.

Line a serving platter with lettuce leaves. Pile the lobster mixture on top. Make a border of alternating egg and tomato slices around the edge of the lobster salad and sprinkle the chives on top. Chill for 1 hour before serving.

SERVES 6

Prawns (shrimp) creole

Metric/Imperial	American
25g/1oz butter	2 tbs. butter
1 small onion, finely chopped	1 small onion, finely chopped
1 small green pepper, cored, seeded and finely chopped	1 small green pepper, cored, seeded and finely chopped
30ml/2 tbs. flour	2 tbs. flour
700g/1lb 7oz canned tomatoes, chopped	1lb 7oz canned tomatoes, chopped
5ml/1 tsp. dried rosemary	1 tsp. dried rosemary
5ml/1 tsp. dried thyme	1 tsp. dried thyme
5ml/1 tsp. dried oregano	1 tsp. dried oregano
5ml/1 tsp. sugar	1 tsp. sugar
250g/8oz peeled prawns	½lb shelled shrimp

Melt the butter in a saucepan. Add the onion and pepper and fry until softened. Sprinkle over the flour and cook, stirring, for 1 minute. Gradually stir in the undrained tomatoes, the herbs, seasoning to taste and sugar. Stir well and simmer gently for 15 minutes or until thickened.

Add the prawns (shrimp) and cook for a further 5 minutes. Serve hot, with boiled rice.

SERVES 4

Italian seafood stew

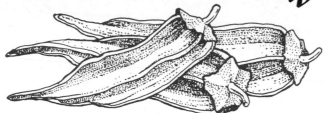

Metric/Imperial	American
120ml/4floz olive oil	½ cup olive oil
2 garlic cloves, chopped	2 garlic cloves, chopped
1 red chilli, seeded and chopped	1 red chili pepper, seeded and chopped
250g/8oz shrimps, shelled and chopped	½lb shrimp, shelled and chopped
250g/8oz squid, chopped	½lb squid, chopped
120ml/4floz dry white wine	½ cup dry white wine
45ml/3 tbs. tomato purée	3 tbs. tomato paste
500ml/16floz water	1 pint water
250g/8oz cod fillet, chopped	½lb cod fillet, chopped
250g/8oz haddock fillet, chopped	½lb haddock fillet, chopped
4 slices of toast	4 slices of toast
1 garlic clove, halved	1 garlic clove, halved
30ml/2 tbs. chopped canned pimiento	2 tbs. chopped canned pimiento

Heat the oil in a saucepan. Add the chopped garlic and chilli (chili pepper) and fry for 5 minutes. Add the shrimps and squid, cover and cook gently for 30 minutes.

Stir in the wine and continue cooking, uncovered, for 15 minutes. Add the tomato purée (paste), water, cod, haddock and salt to taste and mix well. Cover and cook for a further 15 minutes or until the fish is tender.

Meanwhile, rub the toast with the cut sides of the garlic. Place a slice in each serving bowl and ladle over the soup. Garnish with the pimiento.   **SERVES 4**

MEAT

Beef stroganoff

Metric/Imperial
¾-1kg/1½-2lb beef fillet or rump
  steak
75g/3oz butter
2 onions, thinly sliced
250g/8oz mushrooms, sliced
250ml/8floz soured cream
10ml/2 tsp. French mustard

American
1½-2lb boneless beef sirloin
  steak
6 tbs. butter
2 onions, thinly sliced
½lb mushrooms, sliced
1 cup sour cream
2 tsp. French mustard

Cut the steak into strips 5cm/2in long and 5mm/¼in wide.

Melt 50g/2oz (¼ cup) of the butter in a frying pan. Add the onions and fry until softened. Add the mushrooms and cook for a further 3 minutes.

Push the onions and mushrooms to one side and add the steak strips to the pan. Fry, turning, until they are browned on all sides. Mix in the vegetables and add seasoning to taste.

Mix together the sour cream and mustard and stir into the beef mixture. Cook for 1 minute longer, but do not boil. **SERVES 4-6**

Beef & mussel pie

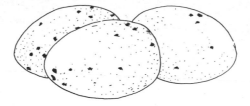

Metric/Imperial	American
50g/2oz butter	¼ cup butter
1kg/2lb lean braising steak, cut into 2.5cm/1in cubes	2lb lean chuck steak, cut into 1in cubes
1 onion, finely chopped	1 onion, finely chopped
2 medium potatoes, diced	2 medium potatoes, diced
250g/8oz mushrooms, sliced	½lb mushrooms, sliced
250ml/8floz dark beer	1 cup dark beer
2.5ml/½ tsp. dried thyme	½ tsp. dried thyme
1 litre/1 quart mussels, steamed and removed from their shells	1 quart mussels, steamed and removed from their shells
250g/8oz frozen puff pastry, thawed	½lb frozen puff pastry, thawed
beaten egg	beaten egg

Preheat the oven to 200°C/400°F, Gas Mark 6.

Melt the butter in a frying pan. Add the steak cubes, in batches, and brown deeply on all sides. Remove the cubes from the pan as they brown.

Add the onion and potatoes to the pan (with more butter if necessary) and fry until the onion is softened. Stir in the mushrooms and fry for a further 3 minutes. Return the steak cubes to the pan and stir in the beer, thyme and seasoning to taste. Bring to the boil, then simmer for 1 hour.

Stir in the mussels and pour the mixture into a 23cm/9in oval or round deep pie dish. Roll out the dough and use to cover the pie. Make a slit in the centre and brush all over with beaten egg. Bake for 50 minutes to 1 hour or until the pastry is risen and golden brown.

SERVES 6

Beef roulade

Metric/Imperial	American
1½kg/3lb braising steak, in one piece	3lb chuck steak, in one piece
175ml/6floz wine vinegar	¾ cup wine vinegar
2 bay leaves	2 bay leaves
6 black peppercorns	6 black peppercorns
3 sage leaves	3 sage leaves
25g/1oz butter	2 tbs. butter
30ml/2 tbs. oil	2 tbs. oil
2 onions, sliced into rings	2 onions, sliced into rings
1 garlic clove, finely chopped	1 garlic clove, finely chopped
4 celery stalks, chopped	4 celery stalks, chopped
1 small turnip, chopped	1 small turnip, chopped
175ml/6floz beef stock	¾ cup beef stock

Cut the meat across the grain into three equal slices. Pound each until thin, then lay flat, overlapping the edges. Roll up and secure with string. Place the meat roll in a shallow dish and pour over the vinegar. Add the bay leaves, peppercorns, sage leaves and 5ml/1 teaspoon salt. Marinate for 2 hours.

Drain the meat roll. Strain the marinade and reserve.

Melt the butter with the oil in a flameproof casserole. Add the meat roll and brown on all sides. Remove it from the pot. Add the onions, garlic, celery and turnip to the casserole and fry until the onions are softened. Return the meat roll to the casserole and pour over the stock and reserved marinade.

Bring to the boil, then cover and simmer for 1½ hours or until the meat roll is tender. Serve cut into thick slices. **SERVES 8**

Beef pot roast with peppers

Metric/Imperial	American
1 x 2kg/4lb top rump of beef	1 x 4lb bottom round of beef
60ml/4 tbs. oil	¼ cup oil
2 large green peppers, cored, seeded and sliced	2 large green peppers, cored, seeded and sliced
2 large red peppers, cored, seeded and sliced	2 large red peppers, cored, seeded and sliced
1 onion, sliced into rings	1 onion, sliced into rings
900ml/1½ pints beef stock	2 pints beef stock
2 garlic cloves, crushed	2 garlic cloves, crushed
2.5ml/½ tsp. dried oregano	½ tsp. dried oregano

Rub the meat all over with salt and pepper. Heat the oil in a flame-proof casserole. Add the meat and brown on all sides. Put half the peppers and all the onion in the casserole and fry until the onion is softened. Stir in the stock, garlic, oregano and seasoning to taste. Bring to the boil, then cover and cook for 2½ to 3 hours or until the meat is tender.

Transfer the meat to a warmed serving platter and keep hot. Strain the cooking liquid and return it to the casserole. Add the remaining peppers and bring the liquid to the boil. Boil for 15 to 20 minutes to reduce well and until the peppers are tender.

Remove the string from the meat and carve it into thick slices. Spoon over the peppers with a little of the liquid and serve the remaining liquid separately as a gravy. **SERVES 6**

Tournedos with herb butter

Metric/Imperial
6 tournedos, about 2.5cm/1in thick
watercress to garnish
Herb butter
75g/3oz butter
15ml/1 tbs. chopped parsley
7.5ml/1½ tsp. lemon juice

American
6 filet mignon, about 1in thick
watercress to garnish
Herb butter
6 tbs. butter
1 tbs. chopped parsley
1½ tsp. lemon juice

First make the butter. Cream the butter until softened, then beat in the parsley, lemon juice and seasoning to taste. Form the butter into a roll, wrap in greaseproof or waxed paper and chill until firm.
Preheat the grill (broiler) to moderately high.
Rub the steaks with salt and pepper and place on the grill (broiler) rack. Cook for about 4 minutes on each side (for rare steaks). Transfer the steaks to a warmed serving platter and top each with a pat of the butter. Garnish with watercress and serve with straw potatoes.

SERVES 6

Boned lamb chops milanaise

Metric/Imperial	American
30ml/2 tbs. oil	2 tbs. oil
1 onion, finely chopped	1 onion, finely chopped
1 garlic clove, crushed	1 garlic clove, crushed
400g/14oz canned tomatoes	14oz canned tomatoes
30ml/2 tbs. tomato purée	2 tbs. tomato paste
1 bay leaf	1 bay leaf
5ml/1 tsp. dried oregano	1 tsp. dried oregano
100g/4oz butter	½ cup butter
50g/2oz mushrooms, sliced	½ cup sliced mushrooms
50g/2oz lean cooked ham, cut into short strips	2 slices lean cooked ham, cut into short strips
250g/8oz spaghetti	½lb spaghetti
8 boned lamb chops (noisettes)	8 boneless lamb chops (noisettes)

Heat the oil in a saucepan. Add the onion and garlic and fry until they are softened. Stir in the undrained tomatoes, tomato purée (paste), bay leaf, seasoning to taste and oregano and bring to the boil. Simmer for 20 minutes. Meanwhile, melt 25g/1oz (2 tablespoons) of the butter in a frying pan. Add the mushrooms and fry for 3 minutes. Stir in the ham and cook for a further 3 minutes. Using a slotted spoon, transfer the mushrooms and ham to the tomato sauce.

Cook the spaghetti in boiling salted water until *al dente*. Drain and return to the saucepan. Stir in 25g/1oz (2 tablespoons) of the butter. Keep warm.

Add the remaining butter to the frying pan and melt it. Add the chops and fry for 4 to 6 minutes on each side or until tender but still slightly pink inside. Transfer to a warmed serving platter, arranging them in a large circle. Pile the spaghetti in the centre and spoon over the tomato sauce.

SERVES 4

Moussaka

Metric/Imperial	American
½kg/1lb aubergines, sliced	1lb eggplants, sliced
25g/1oz butter	2 tbs. butter
1 onion, finely chopped	1 onion, finely chopped
1 garlic clove, crushed	1 garlic clove, crushed
½kg/1lb lean minced lamb	1lb lean ground lamb
4 medium tomatoes, chopped	4 medium tomatoes, chopped
30ml/2 tbs. tomato purée	2 tbs. tomato paste
5ml/1 tsp. dried thyme	1 tsp. dried thyme
45ml/3 tbs. flour	3 tbs. flour
120ml/4floz oil	½ cup oil
300ml/½ pint béchamel or white sauce	1¼ cups béchamel or white sauce
2 egg yolks	2 egg yolks
25g/1oz Parmesan cheese, grated	¼ cup grated Parmesan cheese

Sprinkle the aubergine (eggplant) slices with salt and set aside for 30 minutes.

Preheat the oven to 190°C/375°F, Gas Mark 5.

Melt the butter in a frying pan. Add the onion and garlic and fry until softened. Add the lamb and fry until it loses its pinkness. Stir in the tomatoes, tomato purée (paste), thyme and seasoning to taste and cook for a further 4 minutes. Remove from the heat.

Rinse the aubergine (eggplant) slices and pat dry. Coat them with the flour. Heat a little of the oil in another frying pan and fry the aubergine (eggplant) slices in batches until they are brown on both sides. Add more oil to the pan as necessary.

Cover the bottom of a baking dish with half the aubergine (eggplant) slices. Spoon over the lamb mixture and cover with the remaining aubergine (eggplant) slices. Beat together the béchamel sauce and egg yolks and pour over the top. Sprinkle with the cheese. Bake for 35 to 40 minutes or until the top is lightly browned. **SERVES 4**

Crown roast of pork with peaches

Metric/Imperial	American
1 crown roast of pork, made up of 16 chops	1 crown roast of pork, made up of 16 chops
50g/2oz butter	¼ cup butter
100g/4oz button onions	¼lb pearl onions
½ cucumber, diced	½ cucumber, diced
7 peaches, peeled, halved and stoned	7 peaches, peeled, halved and pitted
60ml/4 tbs. dark treacle	¼ cup molasses

Preheat the oven to 220°C/425°F, Gas Mark 7.

Rub the crown roast all over with salt and pepper. Fill the cavity with crumpled foil and cover the ends of the chop bones with foil. Place in a roasting pan and roast for 20 minutes.

Reduce the temperature to 200°C/400°F, Gas Mark 6 and continue roasting for 40 minutes.

Meanwhile, melt the butter in a saucepan. Add the onions and fry until softened but not brown. Stir in the cucumber. Dice one of the peaches and add to the pan. Cook, stirring, for a further 5 minutes. Remove from the heat.

Remove the foil from the centre of the crown roast and fill the cavity with the onion mixture. Brush the dark treacle (molasses) all over the meat. Arrange the remaining peach halves, cut sides down, in a baking dish and brush with the rest of the dark treacle (molasses). Return the crown roast to the oven with the peaches and continue roasting for 1 hour or until the pork is thoroughly cooked.

Place the crown roast on a serving platter and surround with the peach halves. Remove the foil from the ends of the bones and replace with paper frills.

SERVES 8

Pork & pineapple casserole

Metric/Imperial	American
4 small pork fillets	4 small pork tenderloins
1 garlic clove, halved	1 garlic clove, halved
15ml/1 tbs. grated orange rind	1 tbs. grated orange rind
2.5ml/½ tsp. dried marjoram	½ tsp. dried marjoram
2.5ml/½ tsp. dried sage	½ tsp. dried sage
25g/1oz butter	2 tbs. butter
2 medium green peppers, cored, seeded and shredded	2 medium green peppers, cored, seeded and shredded
300ml/½ pint dry white wine or stock	1¼ cups dry white wine or stock
½kg/1lb canned pineapple rings, drained and chopped	1lb canned pineapple rings, drained and chopped
15ml/1 tbs. cornflour	1 tbs. cornstarch
30ml/2 tbs. orange juice	2 tbs. orange juice

Beat the pork fillets (tenderloins) until flat, then rub all over with the garlic and salt and pepper. Discard the garlic. Sprinkle with the orange rind and herbs and roll up. Tie into shape with string.

Melt the butter in a flameproof casserole. Add the green peppers and fry until softened. Remove them from the casserole. Add the pork rolls to the casserole and brown on all sides. Pour in the wine or stock and add the pineapple and peppers. Stir well and season to taste. Bring to the boil, cover and simmer for 1 hour or until the pork is cooked. Transfer the pork rolls to a warmed serving dish and discard the string. Arrange the green peppers and pineapple around the pork. Keep hot.

Dissolve the cornflour (cornstarch) in the orange juice and stir into the cooking liquid. Simmer, stirring, until thickened. Pour this sauce over the pork and serve. **SERVES 4**

Vitello tonnato

Metric/Imperial	American
1 x 1½kg/3lb boned leg or loin of veal	*1 x 3lb boned leg of loin of veal*
3 anchovy fillets, halved	*3 anchovy fillets, halved*
3 garlic cloves, halved	*3 garlic cloves, halved*
200g/7oz canned tuna fish	*7oz canned tuna fish*
1 onion, thinly sliced	*1 onion, thinly sliced*
2 carrots, sliced	*2 carrots, sliced*
300ml/½ pint veal stock	*1¼ cups veal stock*
175ml/6floz dry white wine	*¾ cup dry white wine*
45ml/3 tbs. wine vinegar	*3 tbs. wine vinegar*
2 bay leaves	*2 bay leaves*
5ml/1 tsp. dried basil	*1 tsp. dried basil*
120ml/4floz mayonnaise	*½ cup mayonnaise*
2 hard-boiled egg yolks, sieved	*2 hard-cooked egg yolks, strained*
45ml/3 tbs. whipped cream	*3 tbs. whipped cream*

Preheat the oven to 180°C/350°F, Gas Mark 4.

Make six incisions in the veal and insert half an anchovy fillet and half a garlic clove in each. Place the veal in a flameproof casserole and add the tuna fish with its oil, the onion, carrots, stock, wine, vinegar, bay leaves, basil and seasoning to taste. Bring to the boil.

Cover the casserole and place it in the oven. Cook for 1½ to 1¾ hours or until the veal is tender. Remove from the oven and cool in the casserole.

Remove the veal from the casserole and carve it into thin slices. Arrange these, overlapping, in a serving platter. Strain the cooking liquid, rubbing as much of the vegetable through as possible, and reserve 250ml/8floz (1 cup). Into this beat the mayonnaise, egg yolks and cream. Pour this sauce over the veal and chill overnight before serving.

SERVES 6-8

Kidneys with sausages & wine

Metric/Imperial	American
50g/2oz butter	¼ cup butter
12 lambs' kidneys, halved	12 lamb kidneys, halved
4 pork chipolata sausages, twisted and halved	4 pork link sausages, twisted and halved
15ml/1 tbs. flour	1 tbs. flour
120ml/4floz red wine	½ cup red wine
250ml/8floz beef stock	1 cup beef stock
15ml/1 tbs. tomato purée	1 tbs. tomato paste
30ml/2 tbs. brandy	2 tbs. brandy
12 button onions, blanched	12 pearl onions, blanched
chopped parsley	chopped parsley

Melt the butter in a frying pan. Add the kidneys and sausages and fry until the kidneys are tender and the sausages brown on all sides. Remove from the pan and keep warm.

Stir the flour into the fat in the pan, then gradually stir in the wine and stock. Bring to the boil. Add the tomato purée (paste), brandy and seasoning to taste and stir well.

Return the kidneys and sausages to the pan with the onions. Mix well, then cover and cook gently for 25 minutes.

Serve hot, sprinkled with parsley.   **SERVES 4**

Chicken fricassée

Metric/Imperial	American
4 chicken quarters	4 chicken quarters
40g/1½oz butter	3 tbs. butter
30ml/2 tbs. oil	2 tbs. oil
2 large onions, chopped	2 large onions, chopped
1 garlic clove, crushed	1 garlic clove, crushed
1 large green pepper, cored, seeded and thinly sliced	1 large green pepper, cored, seeded and thinly sliced
15ml/1 tbs. flour	1 tbs. flour
450ml/¾ pint chicken stock	1 pint chicken stock
60ml/4 tbs. tomato purée	¼ cup tomato paste

Rub the chicken quarters with seasoning to taste. Melt the butter with the oil in a saucepan. Add the chicken quarters, two at a time, and brown on all sides. Remove the chicken quarters from the pan as they brown.

Add the onions and garlic to the pan and fry until softened. Add the green pepper and fry for a further 2 to 3 minutes. Sprinkle over the flour and cook, stirring, until it is golden brown. Gradually stir in the stock and then the tomato purée (paste) and bring to the boil.

Return the chicken quarters to the pan and spoon the liquid over them. Cover and simmer for 1 hour or until the chicken is tender.

SERVES 4

Chicken in white wine

Metric/Imperial	American
8 chicken pieces	8 chicken pieces
25g/1oz butter	2 tbs. butter
2 onions, thinly sliced	2 onions, thinly sliced
250ml/8floz chicken stock	1 cup chicken stock
150ml/¼ pint sparkling white wine	⅔ cup sparkling white wine
2.5ml/½ tsp. dried thyme	½ tsp. dried thyme
1.25ml/¼ tsp. ground mace	¼ tsp. ground mace
45ml/3 tbs. flour	3 tbs. flour
175ml/6floz double cream	¾ cup heavy cream
250g/8oz mushrooms, sliced	½lb mushrooms, sliced
5ml/1 tsp. cornflour	1 tsp. cornstarch
5ml/1 tsp. water	1 tsp. water

Preheat the oven to 220°C/425°F, Gas Mark 7.

Rub the chicken pieces with salt and pepper. Melt the butter in a flameproof casserole. Add the onions and fry until softened. Add the chicken pieces and turn to coat in the butter. Transfer the casserole to the oven and cook for 35 minutes. Remove the casserole from the oven and add the stock, wine, thyme and mace. Sprinkle over the flour and stir vigorously to mix the ingredients together. Warm the cream with the mushrooms without boiling, then add to the casserole. Mix well and bring to the boil on top of the stove. Cover and return to the oven. Cook for a further 40 minutes.

Transfer the chicken pieces to a warmed serving dish and keep hot. Boil the cooking liquid until reduced by one-third. Adjust the seasoning. Dissolve the cornflour (cornstarch) in the water and stir in. Cook, stirring, until thickened, then pour this sauce over the chicken pieces.

SERVES 4

Marbled chicken

Metric/Imperial	American
1 x 1½kg/3lb chicken, boned and slit open	1 x 3lb chicken, boned and slit open
60ml/4 tbs. dry sherry	¼ cup dry sherry
250g/8oz sausagemeat	½lb sausagemeat
100g/4oz salami, sliced	¼lb salami, sliced
100g/4oz pistachio nuts	1 cup pistachio nuts
2 hard-boiled eggs, sliced	2 hard-cooked eggs, sliced
100g/4oz chicken livers, sliced	¼lb chicken livers, sliced
100/4oz mushrooms, sliced	¼lb mushrooms, sliced
1 large red pepper, cored, seeded and sliced	1 large red pepper, cored, seeded and sliced
50g/2oz butter	¼ cup butter

Preheat the oven to 170°C/325°F, Gas Mark 3.

Lay the chicken flat, skin side down, on a sheet of foil. Sprinkle with salt and pepper, then brush with 7.5ml/1½ teaspoons of the sherry. Cover with half the sausagemeat, leaving a 1cm/½in border. Add layers of the salami, pistachio nuts, eggs, chicken livers, mushrooms and red pepper. Top with the remaining sausagemeat. Push the legs inside out so the shape of the chicken is square. Tuck in the wings. Pour over the remaining sherry, then fold over the ends and sides of the chicken to make a neat parcel. Sew the joins with a trussing needle and string.

Dot the chicken with the butter, then wrap in the foil. Put into a roasting pan and cook for 2½ to 3 hours or until the juices that run out of the chicken when it is pierced with a skewer are clear. Cool in the foil and serve cold, in slices.

SERVES 4-6

Spanish chicken

Metric/Imperial
60ml/4 tbs. olive oil
8 chicken pieces
2 onions, thinly sliced
2 garlic cloves, crushed
1 large red pepper, cored,
  seeded and chopped
400g/14oz canned artichoke
  hearts, drained
500ml/16floz chicken stock
1.25ml/¼ tsp. cayenne
1.25ml/¼ tsp. saffron powder
16 stuffed olives, halved

American
¼ cup olive oil
8 chicken pieces
2 onions, thinly sliced
2 garlic cloves, crushed
1 large red pepper, cored,
  seeded and chopped
14oz canned artichoke
  hearts, drained
1 pint chicken stock
¼ tsp. cayenne
¼ tsp. saffron powder
16 stuffed olives, halved

Preheat the oven to 180°C/350°F, Gas Mark 4.
Heat the oil in a frying pan. Add the chicken pieces and brown on all sides. Remove from the pan and place the chicken in a flameproof casserole.
Add the onions, garlic and red pepper to the frying pan and fry until softened. Stir in the artichoke hearts followed by the stock, cayenne, saffron and seasoning to taste. Bring to the boil and pour over the chicken in the casserole. Place the casserole in the oven and cook for 45 to 55 minutes or until the chicken is tender.
Transfer the chicken pieces to a warmed serving dish and keep hot. Boil the cooking liquid to reduce well. Stir in the olives and heat through, then pour this sauce over the chicken. **SERVES 4**

Roast chicken with apricots

Metric/Imperial	American
1kg/2lb canned apricots	*2lb canned apricots*
40g/1½oz butter	*3 tbs. butter*
2 shallots, finely chopped	*2 shallots, finely chopped*
300g/10oz pork sausagemeat	*1¼ cups pork sausagemeat*
15g/½oz fresh breadcrumbs	*¼ cup fresh breadcrumbs*
30ml/2 tbs. double cream	*2 tbs. heavy cream*
5ml/1 tsp. mixed herbs	*1 tsp. mixed herbs*
15ml/1 tbs. chopped toasted	*1 tbs. chopped toasted*
* hazelnuts*	* hazelnuts*
1 x 2.5kg/5lb chicken	*1 x 5lb chicken*
15ml/1 tbs. brown sugar	*1 tbs. brown sugar*
250ml/8floz dry white wine	*1 cup dry white wine*

Drain the apricots, reserving 150ml/¼ pint (⅔ cup) of the can syrup. Chop the apricots finely. Preheat the oven to 220°C/425°F, Gas Mark 7.

Melt 25g/1oz (2 tablespoons) of the butter in a saucepan. Add the shallots and fry until softened. Stir in the sausagemeat and fry until it loses its pinkness. Add the breadcrumbs, cream, herbs, hazelnuts and 30ml/2 tablespoons of the chopped apricots and mix well. Cook gently for a further 5 minutes. Season to taste, then use to stuff the chicken. Truss and rub the chicken all over with salt and pepper. Place it in a roasting pan and roast for 15 minutes.

Meanwhile put the reserved apricot can syrup, sugar, wine and remaining butter in a saucepan and bring to the boil. Add the rest of the apricots and simmer for 5 minutes or until they are beginning to pulp. Rub the mixture through a strainer to make a smooth purée. Pour this over the chicken. Reduce the temperature to 180°C/350°F, Gas Mark 4 and continue roasting for 1¼ to 1½ hours or until the chicken is cooked. Skim any fat from the cooking liquid and serve as a sauce.

SERVES 6

Venison chops

Metric/Imperial	American
4 venison chops	4 venison chops
1 garlic clove, halved	1 garlic clove, halved
60ml/4 tbs. oil	¼ cup oil
175ml/6floz soured cream	¾ cup sour cream
5ml/1 tsp. grated horseradish	1 tsp. grated horseradish
Marinade	**Marinade**
120ml/4floz dry white wine	½ cup dry white wine
60ml/4 tbs. olive oil	¼ cup olive oil
1 onion, thinly sliced	1 onion, thinly sliced
12 black peppercorns	12 black peppercorns
5ml/1 tsp. dried thyme	1 tsp. dried thyme

Mix together the marinade ingredients in a shallow dish. Add the venison chops and marinate for 24 hours, turning occasionally. Remove the chops from the marinade and pat dry. Rub them with the garlic clove and salt and pepper. Discard the garlic. Reserve the marinade.

Heat the oil in a frying pan. Add the chops and brown on both sides. Pour in the marinade and bring to the boil. Cover and simmer for 20 minutes or until the chops are tender. Remove from the heat and cool. Leave the chops to marinate for a further 24 hours.

Return the pan to the heat and bring to the boil. Simmer for 15 minutes.

Transfer the chops to a warmed serving platter. Keep hot. Strain the cooking liquid into a saucepan. Stir in the sour cream and horseradish and heat through gently. Pour this sauce over the chops and serve.

SERVES 4

Jugged hare

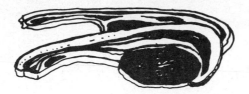

Metric/Imperial	American
50g/2oz flour	*½ cup flour*
1 x 2-2½kg/4-5lb hare, cut into 6 pieces and skinned, blood reserved	*1 x 4-5lb hare, cut into 6 pieces and skinned, blood reserved*
8 streaky bacon rashers, chopped	*8 bacon slices, chopped*
50g/2oz butter	*¼ cup butter*
300ml/½ pint beef stock	*1¼ cups beef stock*
300ml/½ pint dry red wine	*1¼ cups dry red wine*
1 bouquet garni	*1 bouquet garni*
250g/8oz button onions	*½lb pearl onions*
250g/8oz small button mushrooms	*½lb small button mushrooms*
120ml/4floz port wine	*½ cup port wine*

Mix the flour with salt and pepper and use to coat the hare pieces. Preheat the oven to 150°C/300°F, Gas Mark 2.

Fry the bacon in a flameproof casserole until it has rendered most of its fat. Remove the bacon from the pan with a slotted spoon. Add 25g/1oz (2 tablespoons) of the butter to the casserole. When it has melted, add the hare pieces and fry until they are browned on all sides. Stir in the stock and wine and bring to the boil. Add the bouquet garni and seasoning to taste. Cover the casserole and transfer it to the oven. Cook for 2½ hours.

Melt the remaining butter in a saucepan. Add the onions and mushrooms and fry until lightly browned. Add to the casserole with the port. Stir well and cook in the oven for a further 30 to 40 minutes or until the hare is tender.

Place the hare pieces and vegetables in a warmed serving dish. Discard the bouquet garni from the casserole and boil the cooking liquid to reduce. Stir in the reserved blood and cook gently until the sauce is thickened and smooth. Pour over the hare pieces and serve.

SERVES 4-6

Roast pheasant

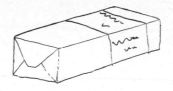

Metric/Imperial
2 young pheasants
50g/2oz butter, melted

American
2 young pheasants
¼ cup butter, melted

Preheat the oven to 180°C/350°F, Gas Mark 4.

Place the trussed pheasants in a roasting pan. Brush with a little of the melted butter and sprinkle with salt and pepper. Roast for 1 hour, basting frequently with more of the melted butter. The pheasants are cooked when the juices run clear when the thigh is pierced with a skewer.

Serve with game chips and bread sauce, garnished with watercress.

SERVES 4

Chestnut Charlotte

Metric/Imperial	American
200ml/⅓ pint milk	⅞ cup milk
150ml/¼ pint water	⅔ cup water
30 sponge fingers	30 ladyfingers
75g/3oz sugar	6 tbs. sugar
15g/½oz gelatine	2 envelopes unflavoured gelatin
160g/5½oz canned unsweetened chestnut purée	5½oz canned unsweetened chestnut purée
30ml/2 tbs. orange liqueur	2 tbs. orange liqueur
100/4oz canned preserved chestnuts	¼lb canned preserved chestnuts
300ml/½ pint double cream	1¼ cups heavy cream

Mix together 75ml/3floz (6 tablespoons) of the milk and water. Dip the sponge fingers (ladyfingers) in to moisten them, then use them to line the sides of a 1.2 litre/2 pint (2½ pint) capacity mould. Trim the ends of the fingers if necessary. Place a circle of greaseproof or waxed paper on the bottom of the mould.

Put the sugar and remaining milk in a saucepan and stir to dissolve the sugar. Heat the remaining water, then add stirring until it is dissolved. Add to the pan with the chestnut purée and liqueur. Mix well. Remove from the heat. Cool, then chill until the mixture is beginning to set.

Drain the preserved chestnuts, reserving the syrup. Chop the chestnuts.

Whip the cream until it is thick and fold it into the chestnut purée mixture with the chopped chestnuts. Spoon into the lined mould. Chill for at least 6 hours or overnight. Turn out to serve, with the reserved chestnut syrup poured over. **SERVES 10**

Orange caramel trifle

Metric/Imperial	American
6 trifle sponge squares, each cut into two layers	12 thin square slices sponge cake
45ml/3 tbs. orange liqueur or sweet sherry	3 tbs. orange liqueur or sweet sherry
45ml/3 tbs. orange juice	3 tbs. orange juice
300g/10oz sugar	1¼ cups sugar
300ml/½ pint thick custard sauce	1¼ cups thick custard sauce
4 large oranges, thinly sliced	4 large oranges, thinly sliced
150ml/¼ pint double cream	⅔ cup heavy cream

Lay the sponge cake squares flat on a tray and sprinkle over the liqueur or sherry and orange juice. Leave for 30 minutes to absorb the liquid.

Melt the sugar in a saucepan, then boil the syrup until it turns golden brown. Remove from the heat and keep warm.

Arrange one-third of the sponge squares in a glass serving dish. Cover with one-third of the custard, then make a layer of one-third of the orange slices. Trickle over one-third of the caramel. Continue making layers in this way, ending with caramel-coated orange slices. Chill for 2 hours.

Whip the cream and pipe stars over the top of the trifle. **SERVES 4-6**

Pears with cardamom

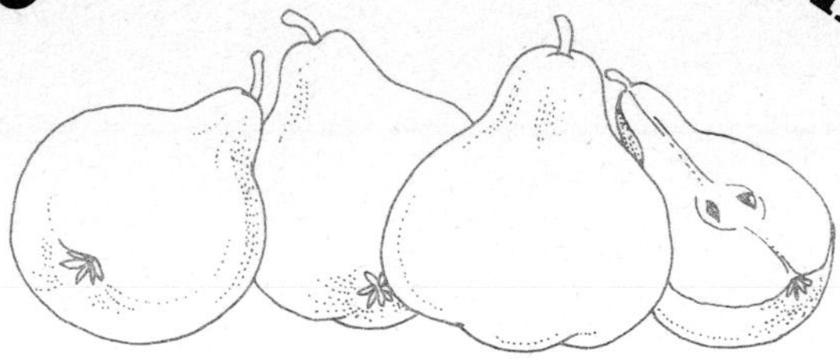

Metric/Imperial

3 large pears, peeled, cored
   and sliced
30ml/2 tbs. brown sugar
120ml/4floz orange liqueur
10ml/2 tsp. ground cardamom
250ml/8floz double cream

American

3 large pears, peeled, cored
   and sliced
2 tbs. brown sugar
½ cup orange liqueur
2 tsp. ground cardamom
1 cup heavy cream

Preheat the oven to 180°C/350°F, Gas Mark 4.

Put the pears in a shallow baking dish. Sprinkle with the sugar, then with the liqueur and cardamom. Bake for 35 to 40 minutes or until the pears are tender. Allow to cool.

Divide the pears and liquid between four serving dishes. Whip the cream and spoon on top.   **SERVES 4**

Peaches with marzipan

Metric/Imperial	American
250g/8oz marzipan	½lb marzipan
250g/8oz sugar	1 cup sugar
350ml/12floz water	1½ cups water
5ml/1 tsp. grated lemon rind	1 tsp. grated lemon rind
4 peaches, peeled, halved and stoned	4 peaches, peeled, halved and pitted
100g/4oz apricot jam	½ cup apricot jam
150ml/¼ pint double cream	⅔ cup heavy cream
30ml/2 tbs. chopped pistachio nuts	2 tbs. chopped pistachio nuts

Preheat the oven to 180°C/350°F, Gas Mark 4.

Roll out the marzipan on a surface sprinkled with cornflour (cornstarch) to about 5mm/¼in thick. Cut out eight 7.5cm/3in circles. Use these to line eight patty tins (shallow muffin pans). Bake for 15 minutes.

Meanwhile, dissolve the sugar in the water in a saucepan. Add the lemon rind and bring to the boil. Add the peach halves and poach gently for 3 to 5 minutes or until just tender. Drain the peach halves. Remove the marzipan cases from the oven and cool.

Heat the jam until it is liquid, then strain it.

Remove the marzipan cases from the tins (pans). Divide the apricot jam between the cases, then place a peach half, cut side up, in each. Whip the cream and pipe in a swirl on each peach half. Decorate with pistachio nuts.

SERVES 4

Rhubarb tart

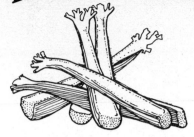

Metric/Imperial	American
100g/4oz sugar	½ cup sugar
250ml/8floz water	1 cup water
½kg/1lb rhubarb, chopped	1lb rhubarb, chopped
2.5ml/½ tsp. ground cinnamon	½ tsp. ground cinnamon
shortcrust pastry made with 250g/8oz flour and 100g/4oz fat	pie pastry made with 2 cups flour and ½ cup fat
beaten egg	beaten egg

Dissolve the sugar in the water in a saucepan. Bring to the boil. Add the rhubarb and cinnamon and return to the boil, then cook gently for 30 minutes or until the rhubarb is very tender. Cool.

Preheat the oven to 180°C/350°F, Gas Mark 4.

Roll out two-thirds of the dough and use to line a 23cm/9in flan tin (tart pan). Spoon the rhubarb mixture into the pastry case.

Roll out the remaining dough to about 5mm/¼in thick and cut into eight strips 1cm/½in wide. Lay these over the rhubarb filling to make a lattice. Brush the dough with beaten egg. Bake for 40 minutes or until the pastry is golden brown. Serve hot or cold. **SERVES 4-6**

Soufflé Grand Marnier

Metric/Imperial	American
100g/4oz caster sugar	$\frac{1}{2}$ cup superfine sugar
5 egg yolks	5 egg yolks
60ml/4 tbs. Grand Marnier	$\frac{1}{4}$ cup Grand Marnier
15ml/1 tbs. grated orange rind	1 tbs. grated orange rind
7 egg whites	7 egg whites
icing sugar	confectioners' sugar

Preheat the oven to 200°C/400°F, Gas Mark 6.

Sprinkle 30ml/2 tablespoons of the sugar over the bottom and sides of a greased 1.5 litre/2$\frac{1}{2}$ pint (1$\frac{1}{2}$ quart) capacity soufflé dish. Put the remaining sugar in a heatproof bowl with the egg yolks. Place the bowl over a pan of hot water and beat until the mixture is thick and pale. Stir in the liqueur and orange rind and remove from the heat. Place the bowl in another bowl filled with ice cubes and stir until cool. Beat the egg whites until stiff. Fold into the egg yolk mixture. Spoon into the soufflé dish.

Place in the oven and reduce the temperature to 190°C/375°F, Gas Mark 5. Bake for 25 to 30 minutes or until risen and golden brown. Sprinkle over a little icing (confectioners') sugar and serve immediately. **SERVES 4-6**

Ice cream peach meringue

Metric/Imperial	American
4 egg whites	*4 egg whites*
250g/8oz icing sugar	*2 cups confectioners' sugar*
apricot jam	*apricot jam*
1 x 23cm/9in sponge cake	*1 x 9in sponge cake*
60ml/4 tbs. orange juice	*¼ cup orange juice*
3 large peaches, peeled, halved	*3 large peaches, peeled, halved*
and stoned	*and pitted*
350ml/12floz sweet white wine	*1½ cups sweet white wine*
6 scoops vanilla ice cream	*6 scoops vanilla ice cream*
60ml/4 tbs. orange liqueur	*¼ cup orange liqueur*

Preheat the oven to 130°C/250°F, Gas Mark ½.

Put the egg whites and sugar in a heatproof bowl placed over a pan of simmering water. Beat until the mixture forms stiff glossy peaks. Remove from the heat and continue beating for 2 minutes.

Draw a 25cm/10in circle on three sheets of non-stick (parchment) paper and place them on baking sheets. Pipe the meringue mixture into one circle to fill it, then pipe rings on the other circles. Bake for 1½ hours or until firm. Cool, then peel off the paper.

Place the meringue base on a flat serving plate. Arrange the rings on top to form the sides of the basket. Secure them with a little apricot jam. Put the cake inside the meringue basket, trimming it if necessary Sprinkle over the orange juice and leave for 30 minutes.

Meanwhile, poach the peach halves in the wine for 15 minutes. Drain and cool.

Soften the ice cream a little and spread it over the cake. Place the peach halves on top, cut sides down. Warm the liqueur and pour it over the peaches. Ignite it and serve while still flaming.   **SERVES 6**

Punch

Metric/Imperial
725ml/1 pint 4floz lemon juice
350g/12oz brown sugar
2 bottles Jamaican rum
1 bottle brandy
1.8 litres/3 pints water
175ml/6floz peach bitters
*250g/8oz peaches, peeled, stoned
  and chopped*

American
1½ pints lemon juice
2 cups brown sugar
2 bottles Jamaican rum
1 bottle brandy
3¾ pints water
¾ cup peach bitters
*½lb peaches, peeled, pitted and
  chopped*

Put the lemon juice and sugar in a punch bowl and stir to dissolve the sugar. Add the remaining ingredients and mix well. Leave for at least 3 hours, stirring occasionally, before serving. **SERVES 36**

RECIPE INDEX

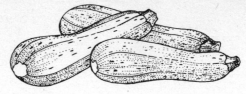